Pg 96

Fact Finders®

EXCEPTIONAL ENGINEERING

EXTRAORDINARY
BUILDINGS

by Izzi Howell

CAPSTONE PRESS
a capstone imprint

Fact Finders Books are published by Capstone Press,
1710 Roe Crest Drive, North Mankato, Minnesota 56003
www.mycapstone.com

Produced for Capstone Publishers by
White-Thomson Publishing Ltd
www.wtpub.co.uk

Library of Congress Cataloging-in-Publication Data
Names: Howell, Izzi, author.
Title: Extraordinary Buildings: The Science of How and Why They Were Built/by Izzi Howell.
Description: North Mankato, Minnesota: Capstone Press, [2019] | Series: Fact Finders. Exceptional Engineering |
   Includes bibliographical references and index. | Audience: Ages 8–10.
Identifiers: LCCN 2018010610 (print) | LCCN 2018013669 (ebook) | ISBN 9781543529050 (library binding) |
   ISBN 9781543529104 (paperback) | ISBN 9781543529142 (eBook PDF)
Subjects: LCSH: Building—Juvenile literature. | Historic buildings—Juvenile literature.
Classification: LCC TH149 (ebook) | LCC TH149 .H69 2019 (print) | DDC 690.09—dc23
LC record available at https://lccn.loc.gov/2018010610

Editorial Credits
Editor: Sonya Newland
Designer: Steve Mead
Media Researcher: Izzi Howell
Production Specialist: Laura Manthe

Photo Credits
Alamy: Sueddeutsche Zeitung Photo, 7, Nancy Hoyt Belcher, 10, James Callaghan, 13; Getty: saiko3p, cover, Keith Myers/Kansas City Star/MCT, 11, oversnap, 12, flavijus, 15, JayLazarin, 17, Exotica.im/UIG, 18, sihasakprachum, 22, Guang Niu, 23, Bettmann, 25t, Marcus Lindstrom, 26, Lars Ternblad, 28, Rfarrarons, 29; Julian Baker: 14, 27; Shutterstock: kerenby, 4, Nickolastock, 5, BNMK0819, 6, kaprik, 8, Jule_Berlin, 9, MISHELLA, 16, CJM Grafx, 19, TonyV3112, 20, Ajancso, 21, R.M. Nunes, 24, Petrovic Igor 25b.

Design elements by Shutterstock.

Printed and bound in the United States of America.
PA021

TABLE OF CONTENTS

CHAPTER 1

HEYDAR ALIYEV CENTER

Many buildings around the world look quite similar. They have a square or rectangular shape with ordinary windows and doors. However, there are some buildings that look quite different. Their extraordinary shapes are fascinating to look at, but they posed unique challenges to the engineers who worked on them.

In the 21st century many new, modern buildings have been built in Baku, the capital city of Azerbaijan. In the 2000s the government decided to build a new cultural center for the country. They named it the Heydar Aliyev Center after a former president of Azerbaijan. A competition was held to find the best design. In 2007 it was announced that the Iraqi-British architect Zaha Hadid and her team had won.

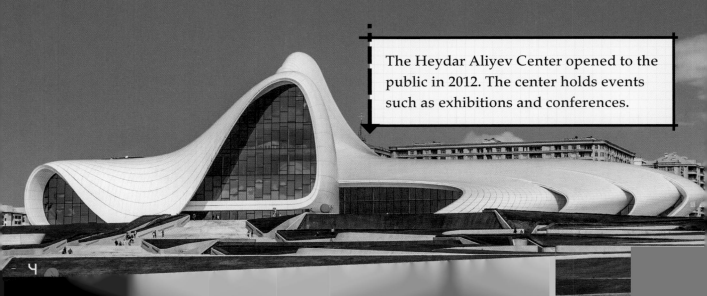

The Heydar Aliyev Center opened to the public in 2012. The center holds events such as exhibitions and conferences.

Zaha Hadid is well known for designing buildings that have **organic**, curved shapes. With the Heydar Aliyev Center, Hadid challenged herself to design a building with no corners. The result is a building with a wavy, folded shape. The folds in the building create different spaces. They give privacy to some rooms and provide large open windows for others.

The fold that comes down in front of this window creates shade and prevents the inside of the building from getting too hot.

organic—free-form and unpredictable; having the appearance of something from the natural world, such as plants, animals, or the sky

Hadid wanted the inside of the building to be open and spacious. She didn't want to have columns inside to support the roof. Instead, the building is made of a lightweight metal **lattice** frame. The lattice is light enough that it doesn't need extra support. The outside of the lattice is covered in very thin pieces of concrete that have been **reinforced** with glass. Each curved concrete panel is different and was made in its own special **mold**.

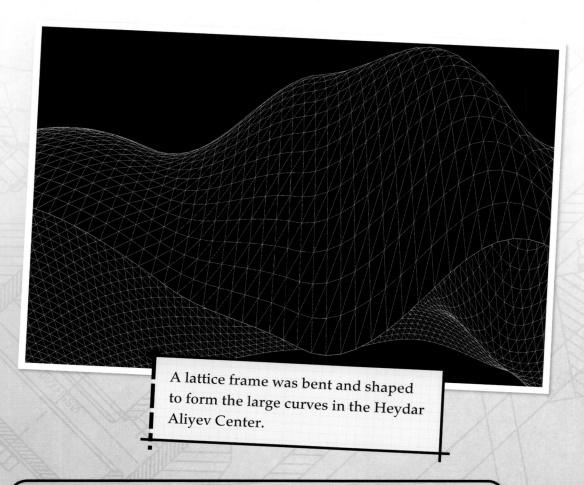

A lattice frame was bent and shaped to form the large curves in the Heydar Aliyev Center.

lattice—a pattern formed by strips that cross each other diagonally
reinforce—to strengthen the structure or shape of something
mold—a model of an object

Hadid and her team used computer programs to design the building and keep track of all the different pieces. Most of the lattice pieces and all of the outside concrete panels were one-of-a-kind, like pieces of a jigsaw puzzle. If one of these pieces had been put in the wrong place, the building wouldn't have stayed up. So it was very important to make sure that the right pieces were put in the correct place.

First the lattice pieces were lifted high into the air by crane. Then workers fitted them into place by hand. The lattice pieces were so thin and light that workers could easily pick them up. Next, the outside panels were laid **parallel** to each other. This made it harder to see the edges between the pieces. It also makes it look as if the building's covering is all one panel.

Workers fit the outside panels to the roof of the Heydar Aliyev Center in 2011.

CHAPTER 2

THE DANCING HOUSE

The Dancing House is a building on the banks of the Vitava River in Prague, Czech Republic. Its name comes from the unusual shape of its towers, which look like a couple dancing. Czech-Croatian architect Vlado Milunić and Canadian architect Frank Gehry teamed up to design the building. Gehry is famous for his **abstract** buildings, such as the Guggenheim Museum in Bilbao, Spain. Construction began in 1994, and the building opened in 1996. Today the building houses a hotel, restaurant, and offices.

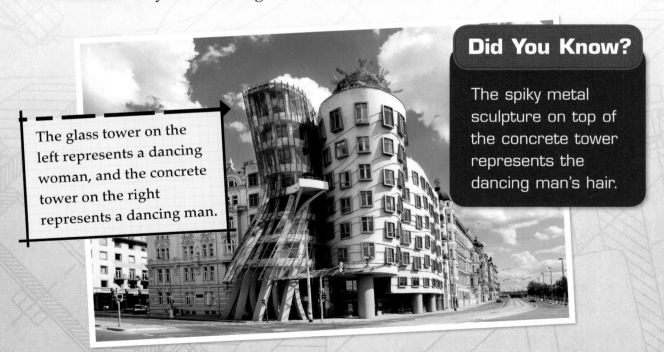

The glass tower on the left represents a dancing woman, and the concrete tower on the right represents a dancing man.

Did You Know?

The spiky metal sculpture on top of the concrete tower represents the dancing man's hair.

abstract—based on ideas rather than things you can touch and see; abstract paintings show impressions rather than what people or objects actually look like

The Dancing House has two parts—a glass tower and a curved concrete section. The outside wall of the glass tower is too **fragile** to hold the building up, so it is supported by pillars inside. The curved concrete section is decorated with thin, wavy lines, which trick the eye into thinking that parts of the wall are bulging out. The windows add to the confusing effect. Their frames stick out, which makes the windows look as if they are coming out of the wall.

The windows on the Dancing House are placed at different heights, which makes the wall look curvy.

EXPERIMENT WITH LOAD-BEARING WALLS

Because the glass wall of the Dancing House is not load-bearing, pillars inside the tower hold the building up. To see how these pillars work, roll a piece of paper into a tube about 2 inches (5 centimeters) in diameter. Secure the tube with a piece of tape, stand it up, and place a heavy book on it. Does the paper hold the book?

Try placing a cardboard tube, such as a toilet paper roll, inside the paper tube. Cut off the top of the paper tube so that it's the same height as the cardboard tube. Does the paper tube support the weight of the book now? This is because the cardboard tube, rather than the paper, is supporting the load.

fragile—easily broken

CHAPTER 3

KANSAS CITY LIBRARY PARKING GARAGE

The parking garage of the Kansas City Public Library in Missouri is easy to spot thanks to the giant books decorating it. When a new garage was needed, the library board asked the community to think of ways to make it look more attractive. They suggested a giant bookshelf that wrapped around the outside of the garage. Kansas City residents sent in ideas for different books to include. The final design shows 22 different book spines, including titles such as *The Wonderful Wizard of Oz* and *The Lord of the Rings*.

Each giant book spine measures 25 feet (7.6 meters) high and 9 feet (2.7 m) across.

The garage beneath the bookshelf is a basic **steel** and concrete structure. The book spines are made from giant mylar sheets. Mylar is a plastic covering that is often used on billboards. Each sheet of mylar was printed with a different design and color scheme to make the bookshelf interesting and eye-catching. Workers used bolts to attach the spines to the garage wall.

The bookshelf was completed in 2004. Eventually the spines may need to be replaced. The mylar sheets are quite fragile, so they will get damaged by the wind and rain over time.

Workers used a special type of **aerial** lift called a cherry picker to reach the top levels of the garage and attach the spines.

Did You Know?

Mylar is used to make many different products, including billboards, measuring tapes, metallic balloons, kites, and the glitter in some types of nail polish.

steel—a hard, strong metal made mostly from iron and carbon
aerial—having to do with things that are high in the air

CHAPTER 4

SELFRIDGES BUILDING

Selfridges is a famous chain of luxury department stores in Great Britain. In the late 1990s, the company decided to open a new store in Birmingham to attract more people to the city. The owners wanted a building that would stand out against the rest of the city center. They chose a **futuristic**, modern design from the architecture firm Future Systems. The building is an example of "blob" architecture, a style in which buildings have organic shapes, like **amoebas**. The building's curved shape and interesting texture make it look more like a sculpture than a building. The building was completed in 2003 and cost $85.5 million.

Visitors enter the building through a glass tunnel that is connected to a parking garage.

futuristic—having a style predicted for the future
amoeba—a microscopic single-celled organism that lives in a wet environment

Workers stood on **scaffolding** to carefully place rows of aluminum discs on the outside of the Selfridges Building.

scaffolding

The structure of the Selfridges Building is made of steel covered in **mesh**. The workers sprayed a thick layer of concrete over the mesh. They used spray concrete because it would have been difficult to build the curved shape from rectangular concrete blocks. A blue covering was then sprayed over the concrete to protect it, and 15,000 aluminum discs were placed on top for decoration.

Did You Know?

The curved shape of the Selfridges Building creates pockets where rainwater could collect. So the architects added hidden **gutters** that sit between the discs to carry water away.

scaffolding—a temporary framework or set of platforms used to support workers and materials

mesh—a woven material made of threads or wires with open spaces between them

gutter—a shallow trough or channel through which rain is carried away from a roof or road

CHAPTER 5

THE OCULUS BUILDING

The World Trade Center Transportation Hub in New York City is a busy underground station where people catch trains from different platforms. Above the station is the stunning Oculus Building. Inside the Oculus is an oval hall around the size of a football field. There are cafés, shops, and ticket machines in the hall. Windows in the Oculus let daylight into the station and down to the platforms below.

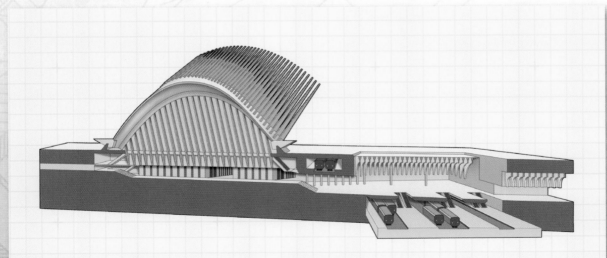

The train and bus stops at the World Trade Center Transportation Hub are underground. Travelers enter the Transportation Hub through the Oculus Building on the ground level.

The original World Trade Center Transportation Hub was destroyed in the terrorist attacks on September 11, 2001. In 2004 New York City's transportation department chose Spanish architect Santiago Calatrava to design the new building for the station. Calatrava is famous for his unusual buildings that look like sculptures. At the top of the Oculus Building are two structures that are meant to look like a bird's wings. These "wings" are made of long steel spikes.

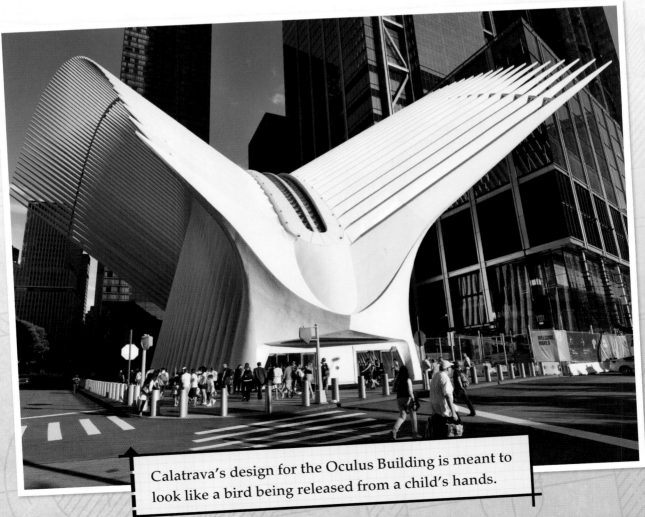

Calatrava's design for the Oculus Building is meant to look like a bird being released from a child's hands.

Between the spikes, thin glass windows let light into the Oculus Building and down to the train platforms 60 feet (18 m) below. A **truss** in the center of the roof helps evenly **distribute** the weight of the building. This is to make sure that there's not too much pressure in one place. Otherwise, the building could cave in.

truss

TEST THE STRENGTH OF TRIANGLES AND SQUARES

The truss in the roof of the Oculus Building is made up of rectangular pieces. This is unusual. Most trusses are made of triangular pieces because triangles are less likely to bend out of shape. Test this with drinking straws and string. Cut three pieces of drinking straw all the same length. Then thread a string through all three pieces and tie in a knot to form a triangle. Repeat with four pieces of drinking straw to create a square.

What happens if you push on one corner of the square? What happens if you push on one corner of the triangle? It is much easier for a square to bend and change shape than a triangle. This is why triangle shapes are often used in construction.

truss—a framework of metal or wooden beams used to support objects, such as bridges, walls, or roofs

distribute—to spread out or divide something evenly

Construction of the Transportation Hub started in 2008. Workers first built the large concrete arches that form the base of the wings and the top of the hall. Then they added spikes to the wings.

Construction of the Transportation Hub took much longer than expected. In addition to the Oculus Building, workers also had to reattach the subway tracks that connect to the station.

The Transportation Hub opened in 2016, two years behind schedule. It cost $4 billion—twice as much as originally planned— making it the most expensive train station in the world.

Workers in cranes added the spikes to the roof of the Oculus Building in 2014.

CHAPTER 6

NATIONAL FISHERIES DEVELOPMENT BOARD

Visitors to the headquarters of the National Fisheries Development Board never doubt that they have come to the right address. The building, which opened in Hyderabad, India in 2012, looks like a giant fish. Despite its creative design, the building is still practical, with room for offices inside.

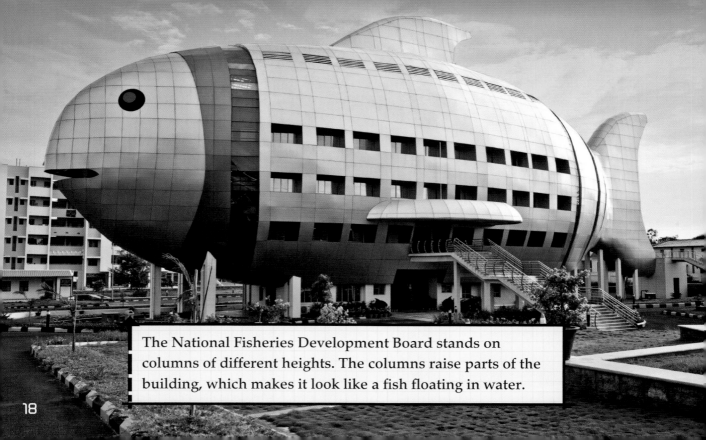

The National Fisheries Development Board stands on columns of different heights. The columns raise parts of the building, which makes it look like a fish floating in water.

The architectural details of the National Fisheries Development Board help make it look more realistic. The stainless steel panels that cover the outside of the building are shiny, just like fish scales. Round windows at the front of the building look like eyes. An awning above the front door resembles a fin. At night, the building is lit up by blue lights, creating an underwater effect.

MIMETIC ARCHITECTURE

The National Fisheries Development Board is an example of mimetic architecture—a style in which a building is designed to look like an object. The design often has something to do with the product the company that owns the building is known for. Another example of mimetic architecture is the former headquarters of the Longaberger Basket Company in Newark, Ohio. This building was constructed to look exactly like the wooden baskets produced by the Longaberger Company.

In winter, the handles of the Longaberger Basket Building can be heated to prevent ice from forming and damaging the structure.

CHAPTER 7

BEIJING NATIONAL STADIUM

Beijing National Stadium in China was designed and built for **track and field** events in the 2008 Summer Olympics. The opening and closing Olympic ceremonies were also held there. The stadium's unusual design has made it a Beijing landmark. It will also be used for events in the 2022 Winter Olympics.

The building's nickname—the Bird's Nest—comes from the design of the stadium's steel roof.

track and field—a group of sporting events that includes running, jumping, and throwing contests, such as hurdles, long jump, pole vault, and shot put

Swiss architects Jacques Herzog and Pierre de Meuron, along with Chinese artist Ai Weiwei, designed Beijing National Stadium. The architects were inspired by the cracks that can form in the **glaze** on Chinese pottery. The plans for the inside of the stadium had to be very precise. There are strict rules about the size of the running tracks for the Olympics, so the ground floor needed to be large enough to fit the track. The designers also had to allow enough space for seating. If the height of the first row of seats had been 4 inches (10 cm) taller, it would have made the whole stadium much larger. It would have also cost millions of dollars more to build.

During the 2008 Summer Olympics, Beijing National Stadium held 91,000 seats.

glaze—a thin coat of liquid that is applied to pottery before it is fired to give it a shiny, colorful finish

21

Beijing National Stadium was designed in two separate parts. The inside of the stadium is a red concrete bowl that contains the seating. The steel roof structure sits on top of the bowl, with a 50-foot (15-m) gap between the two parts. Splitting the building into two separate parts makes it stronger during earthquakes. During an earthquake, each part can move on its own without pulling down the other part.

The steel roof structure looks random and messy, but it was carefully planned. The architects used computer programs to make sure all the different sections fit together properly.

Did You Know?

If you laid the pieces of the roof structure end to end, it would measure 22 miles (36 kilometers). That's about four times the height of Mount Everest.

The seating area gives the stadium a reddish glow when lit up at night.

Construction of Beijing National Stadium began in 2003. Workers were on a tight schedule so the building would be ready for the 2008 Olympics. During the busiest stage of construction, 17,000 people were working on the stadium.

The original design for the stadium had a **retractable** roof. However, this was changed after a roof with a similar design collapsed at an airport. This change made the building safer and also saved time and money. Even so, the stadium wasn't finished until early 2008, just in time for the Olympic Games.

The large heavy roof pieces were lifted into place using cranes in 2006.

retractable—able to be pulled back or opened

CHAPTER 8

CATHEDRAL OF BRASÍLIA

In the 1950s Brazil decided to change its capital from Rio de Janeiro on the coast. They built a new capital city in the center of the country. The new capital city was called Brasília. Because the city was built from scratch, many new important buildings were needed at once. Brazilian architect Oscar Niemeyer was asked to design some government buildings and a new cathedral. His designs for the city had a simple, futuristic style and **geometric** shapes. One of Niemeyer's most famous buildings in the capital city is the Cathedral of Brasília.

The shape of the Cathedral of Brasília represents hands reaching up to heaven.

geometric—having a design that uses simple lines, circles, or squares to form a pattern

Most of the Cathedral of Brasília is actually below street level. The structure that can be seen from the outside is the cathedral's roof. The roof is made of 16 concrete columns, each weighing 90 tons (82 tonnes). The spaces between the columns are filled with windows that let light into the cathedral below.

Work on the cathedral started in 1958. The outside of the cathedral was finished in 1960. But the government didn't have the money to complete the inside of the building or install windows. Eventually the Catholic Church took over and paid for the cathedral to be completed. It opened in 1970.

The Cathedral of Brasília stood unfinished for nearly 10 years.

There are many striking structures in the skyline of Brasília.

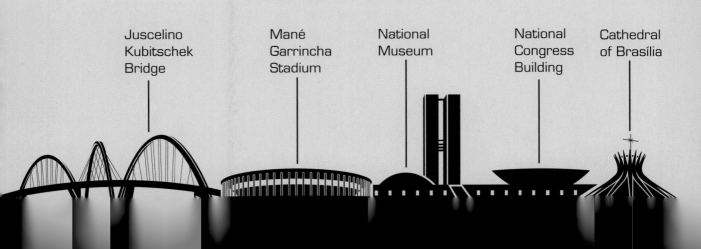

Juscelino Kubitschek Bridge

Mané Garrincha Stadium

National Museum

National Congress Building

Cathedral of Brasília

CHAPTER 9

ERICSSON GLOBE

The Ericsson Globe in Stockholm, Sweden, is a stadium where ice hockey matches and concerts are held. When it was completed, the Ericsson Globe became the world's largest **spherical** building.

Circular windows let small amounts of light into the inside of the building.

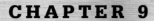

spherical—something with a solid round form like that of a basketball or globe

In the 1980s Stockholm's city council wanted to build a place for sports and cultural events. They held a competition for the best design. They chose a ball-shaped design created by architects Svante Berg and Lars Vretblad.

Berg and Vretblad had never designed a building like this before. But they had an interesting idea about how to build the structure. They designed the inside of the stadium without pillars supporting the roof because they would block the audience's view. Instead, their designs had the outer frame of the building supporting the weight of the domed roof.

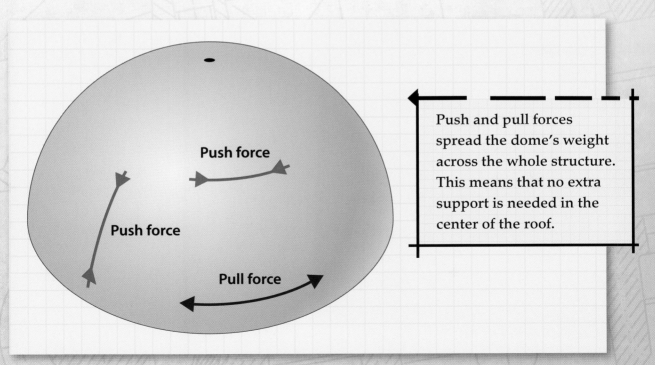

Push force

Push force

Pull force

Push and pull forces spread the dome's weight across the whole structure. This means that no extra support is needed in the center of the roof.

The bottom part of the Ericsson Globe is made up of 48 curved steel pillars. This gives the building a strong base. A thin steel lattice rests on top of the pillars. The lattice is made up of 13,000 steel pipes screwed together with 2,200 joining pieces. It is lightweight, giving the building its spherical shape without needing extra support. The outside of the Ericsson Globe is covered in white aluminum sheets. Depending on the weather and the amount of sunlight, the building seems to change colors. For example, it may appear pink at sunset or gray on a cloudy day.

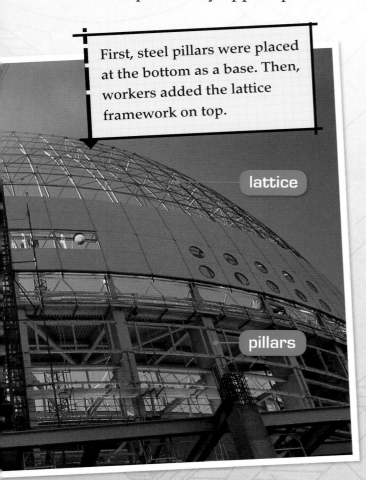

First, steel pillars were placed at the bottom as a base. Then, workers added the lattice framework on top.

lattice

pillars

BUILD AN ARCH

Curved shapes, such as arches and domes, don't need to be supported in the middle. Because the weight is spread across the entire structure, it supports itself. Try building a self-supporting arch using pennies. Start with two stacks. As you add more pennies, make the piles gradually curve toward each other until they meet in the middle.

Construction on the Ericsson Globe started in September 1986. It was finished only two and a half years later in February 1989. In 2010 a new attraction called SkyView opened at the Globe. SkyView is a glass elevator that takes visitors up the outside of the building to the roof of the dome. From the roof—which is 425 feet (130 m) high—visitors have amazing views of Stockholm and the surrounding area.

The tracks of the SkyView elevator weigh 70 tons (64 tonnes). The roof of the Ericsson Globe was reinforced with 42 tons (38 tonnes) of steel supports to carry the weight of the tracks.

GLOSSARY

abstract (ab-STRAKT)—based on ideas rather than things you can touch and see; abstract paintings show impressions rather than what people or objects actually look like

aerial (AIR-ee-uhl)—having to do with things that are high in the air

amoeba (uh-MEE-buh)—a microscopic single-celled organism that lives in a wet environment

distribute (dis-TRI-byoot)—to spread out or divide something evenly

fragile (FRAJ-uhl)—easily broken

futuristic (fyoo-chur-I-stik)—having a style predicted for the future

geometric (jee-uh-MET-rik)—having a design that uses simple lines, circles, or squares to form a pattern

glaze (GLAYZ)—a thin coat of liquid that is applied to pottery before it is fired to give it a shiny, colorful finish

gutter (GUHT-ur)—a shallow trough or channel through which rain is carried away from a roof or road

lattice (LAT-iss)—a pattern formed by strips that cross each other diagonally

mesh (MESH)—a woven material made of threads or wires with open spaces between them

mold (MOHLD)—a model of an object

organic (or-GAN-ik)—free-form and unpredictable; having the appearance of something from the natural world, such as plants, animals, or the sky

parallel (PA-ruh-lel)—an equal distance apart at all points

reinforce (ree-in-FORSS)—to strengthen the structure or shape of something

retractable (ree-TRAK-tuh-buhl)—able to be pulled back or opened

scaffolding (SKAF-uhl-ding)—a temporary framework or set of platforms used to support workers and materials

spherical (SFEER-i-kuhl)—something with a solid round form like that of a basketball or globe

steel (STEEL)—a hard, strong metal made mostly from iron and carbon

track and field (TRAK AND FEELD)—a group of sporting events that includes running, jumping, and throwing contests, such as hurdles, long jump, pole vault, and shot put

truss (TRUHSS)—a framework of metal or wooden beams used to support objects, such as bridges, walls, or roofs

READ MORE

Enz, Tammy. *Building Projects for Beginners: 4D An Augmented Reading Experience*. Junior Makers 4D. North Mankato, Minn.: Capstone Press, 2018.

Hearst, Michael. *Curious Constructions: A Peculiar Portfolio of Fifty Fascinating Structures*. Uncommon Compendiums. San Francisco, Calif.: Chronicle Books, 2017.

Howell, Izzi. *Buildings*. Adventures in STEAM. North Mankato, Minn.: Capstone Press, 2019.

Schmermund, Elizabeth. *Architecture: Cool Women Who Design Structures*. Girls in Science. White River Junction, Vt.: Nomad Press, 2018.

INTERNET SITES

Use FactHound to find Internet sites related to this book.

Visit www.facthound.com

Type in this code: 9781543529050

Check out projects, games and lots more at
www.capstonekids.com

CRITICAL THINKING QUESTIONS

1. What are some different construction methods for building curved buildings? Use details from the text to support your answer.

2. How do architects create large open spaces inside buildings without support in the center? Find evidence in the text to support your answer.

3. How closely do these buildings resemble the architect's original inspiration?

INDEX